All the Pretty Things
Are Dying

poems by

Laurel Maxwell

Finishing Line Press
Georgetown, Kentucky

All the Pretty Things Are Dying

ACKNOWLEDGMENTS

Phren-Z- "What I Carry," "In the News"

Publisher: Leah Huete de Maines
Editor: Christen Kincaid
Cover Art: Laurel Maxwell
Author Photo: eeman agrama, My Own Beat Photography
Cover Design: Elizabeth Maines McCleavy

Order online: www.finishinglinepress.com
also available on amazon.com

Author inquiries and mail orders:
Finishing Line Press
PO Box 1626
Georgetown, Kentucky 40324
USA

Contents

In a Time of Certainty

After Ilya Kaminsky's In a Time of Peace

Inhabitant of this earth for thirty something years
I once found myself in a time of certainty. I watch numbers elevate
and the long lines for nasal swabs. The rush to buy masks and non-
existent at home kits. When a person goes to pay rent, the landlord
takes the keys. Into his hands. Closes.

It is a time of certainty.

When the river rushes backwards, and it is the hottest year on record
for the fifth straight year.
When we pray for rainclouds as fires burn longer,
as starfish no longer regrow their spindly arms.

In this time of certainty we connect over screens and heart emojis.

We see it in the rise of stock for Zoom and Google
the separation
of the whole nation.

We watch. Watch
others watch.

Seeing a pixelated face is exactly like seeing a pixelated face.

It is a time of certainty.

And it displaces our normal
leisurely, the way a white man can shoot a gun.

All of us have to do the hard work of moving forward,
of remembering what it is like to feel the patter of raindrops,
the beauty of regrowth.

This is a time of certainty.

I do not see homelessness,

but watch ducks as they float on the river. How green are the
riverbanks
as water rushes seaward.
How green are the riverbanks (forgive me) how green.

Eight

One night at dinner we asked our waiter about the meaning of life.
"Eight" he replied as he balanced a water jug, plates layering
his elbows like scales.
Eight sideways is infinity.
Is that what he meant?
That life can be infinite if we slow down.
Taste its bitterness and savor those nectar-like moments
The bird hopping for crumbs in slow circles.
My nephew bending and rising like a puppet from the picnic table
with seemingly no other reason
than to laugh at his own silliness.
I've heard it said you either believe in something
or you believe in nothing.
What about those unbelieving unbelievers who hunger?
Who know the universe is grand and they are but a speck of sand.
Those who realize how wide the world spreads and desire
a pocket to claim?
What about the pelicans who coast overhead?
What about the bumblebees waiting for the flowers
to turn in full to the sun?
What about the waves that continually somersault onto the shore?
There must be some magic in the world still.
Some reason to wake in the morning. To buy bread at the store.
To pull on socks and jeans and step into the threshold of existence.
I have no illusions that I've found the reason yet.
And I'll go on wondering with each mundane moment
of breath and breeze.
And I'll ask each person I meet if they know the answer.
And I'll even ask the stars.
Even though I know they will outlive me, in fact already have.
And I'll ask pushing through my doubt of a reply.
Even as the whales migrate and the temperatures rise.
Even as the salmon spawn and strawberries ripen on the vine.

In the News

Most of those on the platform were women and children who had waited outside for hours in falling snow and freezing temperatures...   *–CNN*

We spent the early March afternoon in the garden
shoveling dirt into a large sieve collecting rocks, terra cotta pieces,
shards of glass.
Even after an hour of rain the ground was still too dry.
We uncoiled the hose and watched as the ground soaked in needed moisture.
In our fingers was the itch of distraction.
As WWIII erupted a continent away, with too many tasks and not
enough time for completion, the loss of colleagues to
balance the books.
Repetition expanding like a fun house mirror
we no longer chose to look at.
Dirt slid under fingernails as worms crawled over our thumbs
happily excreting nutrients.
As the sun glared, we thoughtlessly threw our jackets on the cement
path between the beds growing sweet peas, tobacco, nasturtiums.
Patted the soil around chard and lettuce.
Work we could become lost in.
Where it wasn't necessary to say anything besides
"pass the shovel."

Bottled Hearts

Tell me, where do broken hearts go?
Those pieces scattered on the ground like deflated confetti.
Each half turned away from the other in the cavity of our chests.
Like lovers sleep gone sour.
And still the body lumbers into wakefulness.
Brushes teeth, presses the button on the coffeemaker.
Looks out the window to the trees tangling vines on rooftops.
I think of Kintsugi.
Repairing myriad cracks with gold.
Is that how the heart keeps from grieving?
Continually remaking itself until it has become
something else altogether?
Becoming worthy of attention even as it has lost
pieces of itself in the shattering.
Those broken elements so often discarded in the basement of souls.
What happened to second chances?
Starfish regrow limbs.
Why then can humans not regrow the branches to their hearts?
Instead they wall and construct.
Is it no wonder then that as a species we are so lonely?
The moon has the stars.
The clouds have rain.
Flowers their petals.
And what do humans have?
All these washed-up hearts bottled and broken.

When Happiness Meets with Sorrow

Those days, dark as you imagine the depths of the ocean.
Swirling in the loneliness of your own desperation.
It is a miracle you can get out of bed and pour a cup of coffee.
Even then, that takes most of the days effort.
Glancing out the window is the farthest escape you know
how to obtain.
The meetings where you chart your happiness and color
outside the lines.
An attempt to gain part of you gone missing.
When you dragged your feet returning home.
To what?
An absent husband. Dust on the windowsill.
The tunnel stretching further from the light.

And then years pass and you're making bread.
A recipe shared for generations.
Proof the yeast. Stir in the olive oil.
Sprinkle of salt. Pinch of sugar.
You're tumbling the dough onto itself. And you are content.
Your husband is asking for your favorite song for
the evening's backdrop.
And this is the moment you've been yearning for,
each minute encased in amber gold
crystalizing and hardening into memory.

It continues. Our hurts familiar
as the loose porch step, the grease stains
on the kitchen cupboards.
We live with all this hard knowing-
bombs blasting Ukraine, the drought,
and right now another mother is grieving
the loss of her brown son to violence or lock up.
After our heart remakes itself, we close the browser
and kiss loved ones to safety.

How do we do it? How do we want
to make bread again? The punch and the rise,
forming the dough into a ball. How does belief
keep ballooning in the stillness of our soul,
how do these heartbeats hold so much battered
hope in humanity?

I open the oven, place
the bread to cool. All I have grieved
on the counter. I sweep
the contents into my palms.

Worry

I worried when the rains didn't come.
I worried when it seemed the rains wouldn't stop.
I worried when they said costal fogs will no longer
mist redwood needles.
I worry my young niece and nephews won't know about polar bears
and clean air.
So much in their lifetime is already disappearing.
I worry we have forgotten how to love.
That we have become lost in the orbit of ourselves.
I worry communication has become one sided- full of anger and
righteousness.
I worry about the disappearing bees and birds that swallow balled
bits of Styrofoam.
I worry about the starfish who are already losing their limbs.
I worry about the homeless along the riverbank when it floods.
I worry when there have not been eggs at the store for weeks.
I worry we will forever live in mindsets deficit.
I worry there is too much silence weighted by fear.
I worry we are hurtling toward "normal" without understanding what
we have lost.
I worry we will forget to say what we mean.
I worry about how money in the bank so quickly disappears.
I worry we are all searching for something which no longer exists.
I worry these worries, once exposed will never cease.
I worry we will all become too lonely to notice each other's loneliness.
I worry nobody will hold my hand.
I worry we will take more than we can give.
I worry there will be nothing left.
I worry the seas will continue to rise, the rivers to flood.
And there is nothing we can do to prevent it.
I worry we have already lost our way.
Devoured the crumbs to find our way home.

Warning

I've been thinking about hummingbirds.
How they flit and flutter with their needle-like beaks.
How they dip in and out of blooms as if they were making love.
"*Pica y se fue*" my host mom once told me.
They bite and leave.
Except she was talking about the way men make love.
Only being able to handle so much of a woman.
Each hummingbird crafted for a certain flower.
Humans attempt to push square pegs through round circles.
How we dam rivers and clear-cut forests
while in the same breath exclaim about the extinction of species.
This morning walking on the beach I saw a halibut
with its skyward eye pecked out.
Two feet away a seal languidly lounged in the surf.
Now the "back to the land movement" is remerging.
But hasn't land always been something occupied by humans?
And by occupied I mean stripped, mined, fracked, dredged, drained,
desolate, destroyed, diverted.
All so we can proclaim progress.
The ocean only wants to whisper onto the sand.
Trees want to root and shoot like arrows to the azure sky.
Seagulls to scavenge.
Flowers to sunbathe in the sun.
That hummingbird, when it turned its head
showed a swath of red feathers.
So bright.
It was almost a warning.

Destruct

On November 2018, the Camp Fire burned 153,336 acres in Butte County, California. To date it has been the deadliest and most destructive fire in California's history.

Unaware, I arrive in a burnt forest
and stroll slowly, my limbs moving
heavily inspect scarred trunks,
what remains of foundations,
the view is clear because no branches obstruct
it, this forest, this sky, this forest,
I have on my face the opposite of
awe, that humans
destruct, heartsick I hide hopelessness
and despair because this is our home,
and I don't know whatever
you will survive this devastation, universe.

Ocean's Lament

How have you been so ignorant as to not hear the complaints in my
crash and boom which echo off sandstone cliffs?
The continual plea made in the rise and fall of each wave
hitting the sand hard as a fist.
It is no wonder I become so angry some days.
Like a mood ring I wear my emotions on the surface.
Energizing emerald
Trustworthy turquoise
Insecure swirl of brown eddies
Withdrawn in waves of grey.
You, humanity have changed me beyond recognition.
With your sea walls and rip-rap, your wharfs and docks,
your sewage drained into the tide line.
Like children you clamor for your treasures- squid, crabs,
blue fin tuna.
Catch them up in your nets and dump them shimmering onto slick
decks. Toss the unwanted back one by one.
Tell me, could you foresee your own destruction?
Tides licking doorsteps with their slippery tongues, floating in water
which once numbed toes.
Kelp strangled in the whir of motorboat propellers.
Particles of swirling plastic.
Starfish with lost limbs.
Coral bleached of their rainbow colors.
You couldn't blame me for wanting to swallow your towns like Jonah.
As you continue to destroy me with your human needs
did I ever wish I had not receded?
Kept valleys full of microorganisms and vertebrae
that extinguish like stars.

Birds Return

The birds returned first
after that summer. When

 fires smothered the sky
like a thick, brown blanket.

As we became scuba divers
breathing stale air.

RVs sitting in driveways
melted into puddles of metal.

Our home, a fortress surround by
the muddy river.

And still, we waited.
As green nylon tents filled

 high school gymnasiums,
civic centers, fairgrounds.

Mountain communities flooded
back roads.
Into cities which would hold them.

The fire roared
 through canyons. Picked up

speed in its relay to the ocean.
 Water hurriedly dropped from fire crews

sent from Washington, Australia, Oregon.
Six months later rivers of mud

poured down denuded mountains.
The ones we hiked years ago

with your siblings one summer. Where
one sister found a six pack of beer

behind our campsite. Where
the other walked to the camp store

every evening for ice cream. Where a
soon to be ex-boyfriend pouted

on the beach.
Thirty miles through the towering redwoods

to the wild sea.
Now unfamiliar as the clear air

we hungered for. The place we began
burnt and charred as a smoker's lung.

A colleague broke the fire line to save his chickens.
Plucked one at a time from the hen house.

Tucked tenderly between cardboard boxes of clothes.
His son's baseball glove.

Their pastel-colored eggs an offering
within his blackened palms.

St. Nothing

It is hard to believe in humanity when all it does
is throw grenades at feelings.
Not even patient enough to wait for the aftermath.
When news scares rather than informs.
Is it no wonder we choose to stay indoors?
The rotating earth doesn't care about human greed.
It most likely (hopefully) will be here long after humans
are absent from its sphere.
Today I read about a star eating its planet.
Even space has its hungers.
Once the star had swallowed its orb it began to shine brighter
taking energy from its meal.
Maybe wonder then is something to believe in.
The way after eons of removal buffalo return to familiar migration
patterns.
That trees communicate through their crowns.
Mycelium with their underground network of signals.
The flower dropped by an unassuming bird growing in the drainpipe.
Its purple bobbing startling me into curiosity one ordinary morning.
The wonder is that there is life at all left
on this concrete studded planet.
After all we have learned to survive.
Breath held, hands clenched.
Wonder what will be there when we awake in the morning.

Natures Desires

We are still perfecting the desires.
After we have lost them among gigabytes, iphones, the world wide
web.
The desire perhaps to unplug from ourselves for just a moment.
Shut down Instagram, close the browser, close the tabs, gently close
the lid. Fold itself onto sticky keyboards.
And what is it we so desire in the world?
Its possible only a cup of coffee, a warm bed, a
bouquet of flowers blooming on the table.
Its possible we want something deeper.
Loneliness has become an epidemic.
Killing more people than smoking.
Facetime can only bring a face so close.
It's possible sometimes we desire touch.
The grubby hand of a child, the smooth palm of a lover,
the warm embrace of an acquaintance.
Can we eat our desires with a simple fork and spoon?
If swallowed, would they bloom- dandelions in our stomachs?
What if we caught them with a net?
Picked them off the bottom of our shoe?
We so often say there will be time for curiosity.
I'm not sure I believe that lie.
So often our days are filled with screens that tell us
what to think and feel.
What to buy and consume.
This cream or that. This cast-iron skillet.
This new best thing that will make you happy for a moment longer.
When the sky is so blue.
And the birds are drifting on drafts above the trees.
Purple buds emerging on branches.
The creek stilling for summers rush.

Ode to Praise

Praise the garden—its tender tendrils of snap peas.
The gritty skin of a plump summertime tomato.
Brown leaves of the potato plant which say "dig."
Praise the bees that buzz their way between the purple basil bush,
umbrella leaves of squash.
Pollinating without thought.
Praise the tools of the gardener. Spade, hose, hat. Gloves
tossed aside.
In order to feel something alive sift against palm lines and stick
under fingernails. A desire to
return ourselves to the earth.
Praise routine. Providing an outline to the shadow of days.
Heft the blue bag over one shoulder, click the door shut.
Walk the half block down the one-way street.
Through the aqua gate with the old man on the bench.
Nodding his head with a *buenas tardes.*
Stalks of sunflowers rupture from the dirt as berries
trail the crooked fence line.
Praise patience without timeline or judgment.
The ability to unwind ourselves from past mistakes.
Make believe humanity has a kernel of kindness.
Praise the body which knows how to lift and twist. Forever falling
and picking itself up
as if it were a form of flight.
Praise our desire for wings.
Not so that we fly too close to the sun.
But so we can marvel at our unique smallness
in the grandness of the universe.

Week

While last week
I'd forgotten already the
names of people I'd met.
Already let their names dissipate into the foggy air.
Already let the trash sit still one more day.
Are there ways to search the streets for joy?
As the roses tip skyward.
As poppy petals fold onto themselves like wings.
The vines that climb the trellis.
A drop of water quivering on the faucet before it
beads and drops.
How close are we to times of sweetness and disaster?
How planets hurtle themselves through space without
knowing their outcome.
How there is always more we wish we'd said.
How there is never enough time.
And geese honk overhead.
And a lake ripples outwards.
And black bark becomes soft duff.
As birds tug worms from wet soil.
And I wonder if the world will still for just a moment.
So we can all remember how to breathe.
To let air fly from our open mouths and be carried by the breeze.

What I Carry

What do you carry?
Regret in my brow and the droop of my eyelids.

What do you carry?
This life like an anchor.

Who carries this weight?
My heart, my knees, the inside of my elbows.

What would you do with lightness?
Throw it into the air like confetti and watch it fall like child's innocent laughter.

Where is the best place to keep regret?
They all say to tuck it away like a bedsheet. I believe it is best out in the open like smoke that clings to jackets, the tendrils of hair follicles.

How do you tally regret?
With pen and paper, with broken hearts, an empty tube of toothpaste.

Is regret hungry?
It is never satisfied with what it has.

How do you keep it full?
With lies of omission.

When do you let it go?
When it becomes too heavy to carry.

How often is that?
I have lost count of the ways I have set it down and walked away, the wind licking my back like a cherry lollipop.

Is regret sweet?
I have lost my ability to taste anything but bitterness.

Then how do you live?
Unfolding like a flower that turns its head to the sun.

Self-Love

After Naomi Shihab Nye's Kindness

Before you sense what self-love really is
you must kindle thoughts,
know that you are worth the space you take up in the world.
Not the silent space of scumbling to others
but the space that is wild as a field of untamed horses
whose manes untangle with the whip of wind.
How you sink and sink
thinking the current will never still,
the spawning salmon
will flash by forever.
Before you learn the tender solace of self-love,
you must visit the empty house
hidden by tall grasses.
You must see how this could be you,
the house too was something loved
who housed a people with hearts and desires
and the simple need to belong.

Before you know self-love as the tenderest thing
you must know loneliness as the other tenderest thing.
You must wake up with loneliness.
You must listen to it till your voice
swallows the root of all loneliness
and you hear the echo of its symphony.

Then it is only self-love makes sense anymore
only self-love that takes your hand
and leads you out into the day to inspect the air
only self-love that peers
from the porch of the world to say,
It is I you have been wishing for
and then wanders with you everywhere
like an image or a smile.

Heartburn

After Aida Limon

Three homes burned in a wild-fire.
There. That is the hard part.
I wanted to tell you so we could
grieve together. So many lost things,
that is just one on a long, current list that
carries forwards and backwards, ripples over stones, logs moss-slick.
What is it they say, lost heart?
I picture a heart standing at the crossroads in a forest
with a map and compass, tracing a careful line
over the folds and creases while looking into identical horizons
thinking this confusion will
orient itself (it rarely does).
The heart is creating a lifeline
and aching and remaking all the sweet
parts of her that have gone sour.
The heart is so tired of carrying
itself, she wants to lay herself down
but also she wants the wind to turn,
wants the smoke to clear.
What the heart wants? The heart wants
her home back.

Monarch

After Mary Oliver's Wild Geese

You do not have to be brave.
You do not have to walk
through the night of the forest searching.
You only have to let the hard corners of your mind
open to what it needs.
Tell me about hope, yours, and I will tell you mine.
Meanwhile the day goes on.
Meanwhile the golden leaves and the outline of clouds
are moving across the road,
over the ocean and deep valleys,
the bayous and the grasslands.
Meanwhile the monarch, fluttering in the clear blue sky
are forwarding toward trees again.
Whoever you are, no matter how distraught,
the world offers itself to your conscience,
distracts you like the monarch, gentle and humble
moment by moment marking your migration
in the soft undercurrent of air.

Patience

Do the flowers wait for the bees to load their
legs with pollen before taking flight?
Do the larva of a butterfly count the seconds until
their wings burst forth like a flag of nature?
Maybe patience is watching green shoots pop up from
damp soil. Waiting to pick the first golden globe
of summer and plop it into your mouth. It's
gritty yellow skin lush against your teeth.
Patience could be trying to mediate while cars slow
like ants in honey on a one lane road.
The tangle of sweet pea vines in their explosion of lavender and rose
take months
to top the trellis.
Lions will stalk as long as they need before they
take their prey.
It takes cicadas seventeen years to arise in swarms
and settle into tree branches.
All that waiting for only a mere decade of living.

End's Beginning

It is said everything must come to an end.
The flowers loose their blooms, the rain retracts into the downy
pillow of clouds which wisp across the sky.

And still the body knows how to move limber and lithe as branches
that sway without breaking.
Did you know the human heart weighs less than a pound?

The heart of a whale weighs three hundred tons.
Mammals both who sing their sad songs in the underwater
underworld of existence.

The wavelength of lonely calls that revibrate across the empty
chambers of the heart.
Today the muddy river overflowed its banks washing across the
footpath we transverse daily going from here to there.

Logs bobbed on their way to the sea next to one lost sandal, a
basketball, a few dozen tree stumps.
We could hear the roar from our open window.

The earth so saturated after years of drought it belched up all the
water which continued to fall.
So much of what we carry is precious.

Our anchor of emotions, the balloon of hope in our chests.
Our rainbow arc of desire.

The only thing which is certain is our mortality. Even birth is
precarious.
An orchid will drop it's petals over the course of a few months, lilies
regrow their shoots without a glance.

Their one-day pop of color will remind us that they too are alive.
So we let dirt collect under our fingernails and reduce the bank
account to zero, mold bloom in spots on the ceiling.

Salmon spawn backwards to the sea while humans hurry themselves
forever forward.
The race to death's finish line.

Tell me, what is the rush to reach the path in the stars so rapidly?

When earth delights in the earthworm and spiderweb.
When there is so much we will never know.

Laurel Maxwell is a writer and poet from Santa Cruz, CA. Her work draws inspiration from the natural world and is moved by the ways people interact with a changing climate. Her work has appeared at *baseballballard.com*, *coffecontrails*, *phren-z*, *Verse-Virtual*, *Tulip Tree Review*, and *Yellow Arrow Vignette*. She also blogs about travel and teaching. She holds a B.A from Whitworth University and served as a Peace Corps Volunteer in the Dominican Republic. She works in education and loves to get lost in bookshops.